USBORNE
Big Picture Book
LONG AGO

Laura Cowan & Sam Baer

Illustrated by Wesley Robins

Designed by Jamie Ball & Helen Lee

Hello! Welcome to our city!

Turn the pages to see what life was like in my time.

And mine!

And ours!

And in our time — before there even was a city!

BUSY CITY

This is the middle of the city nearly 100 years ago.
It's similar to today: there are people going to work,
people shopping, cars and buses on the streets.
But look more closely. See what looks different.

Then turn to the next page to go back in time.

PLEASURE GARDENS

The city was smaller 250 years ago, but it was still busy. People who could afford to pay the entrance fee escaped to nearby pleasure gardens to relax in the day and have fun at night.

Castle ruins

Ooo!

Aaa!

No one ever beats me at cards.

The party tonight is called a masquerade ball.

SPLISH

Lots of people wear masks and costumes.

I want a dancing dog!

I don't think they're for sale.

Acrobat

This is Mr. Drury. He owns the garden.

It's a pleasure to meet you.

I can sing you the music before you buy it.

Ballad seller

To the city
Thieves sneaking in
Mi mi mi mi!
Orchestra
PARP!
I'll light your way, lady.
Big, white wigs are the height of fashion.
There's a bird in my wig!
This music is magnificent! Who wrote it?
Handel, of course.
Your dessert, madam.
Why are there so many fruit puddings? Where's the chocolate mousse?
What a rude man!
First I powder my face all white and then I put rouge on my cheeks.
People gossip about each other behind their fans.
Oy, you! Show me your ticket.
Oh... er...
Not everyone has paid to get in tonight.

MARKET DAY

Nearly 350 years ago, the market was the busiest part of the city. People came in from the countryside to buy and sell things, and catch up with the news.

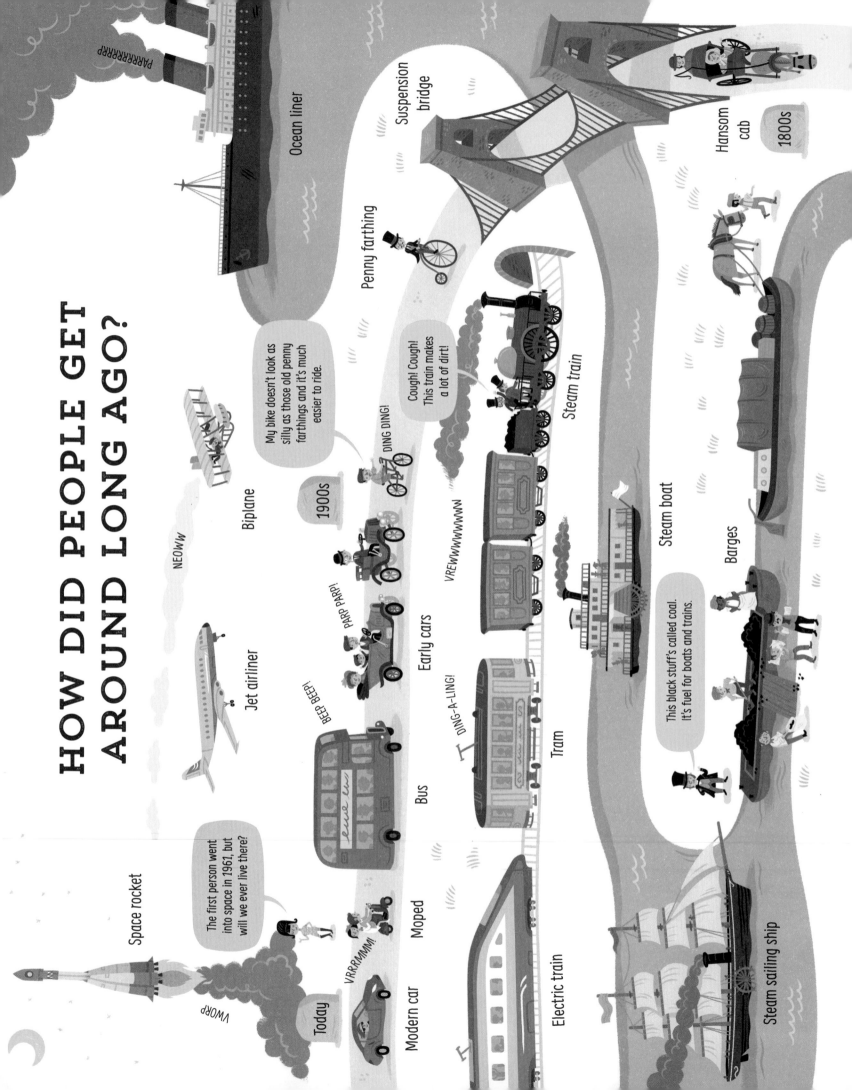

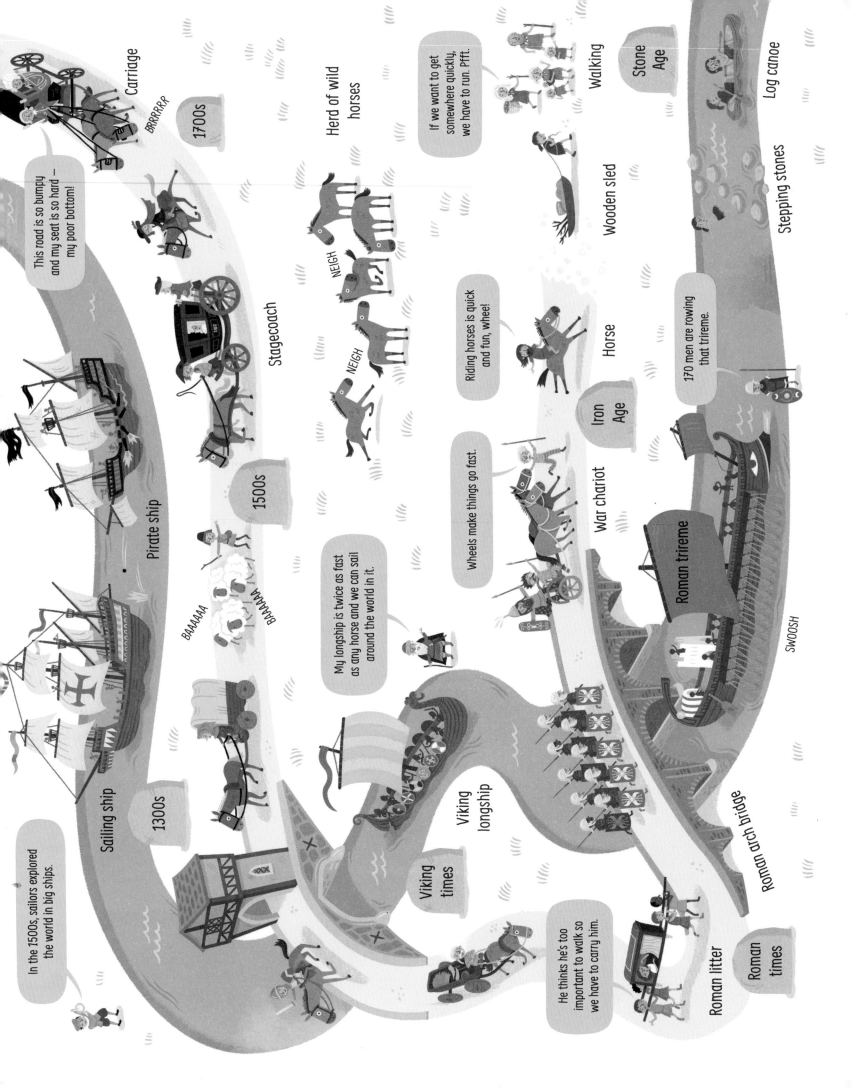

UNIVERSITY

Around 550 years ago, the city's university was growing, as students came from all over the country to study here. Printing presses were a new invention allowing more books to be made than ever before.

Student lodgings

Splish splash

Artist's studio

If the prince likes this portrait I might get to paint him next.

Lecture hall

Making paper

Just going to add to some more wet rags to this frame...

So then we press the water out of the frame and when it's dry we'll have paper.

Printing books

Put the letters in this grid.

Printing books is much quicker than copying them out by hand — the old-fashioned way.

I sing of love!

Run! The statue's falling!

REOW!!

SNAP

Treadmill crane

Learning about the human body

Library

Copying out ancient texts by hand

Band of musicians paid for by the city

BUILDING A CATHEDRAL

Nearly 1,000 years ago, the city was just a small town. A huge, towering church, called a cathedral, was being built. When it was finished, people came from miles around to pray here.

WHAT DID PEOPLE WEAR LONG AGO?

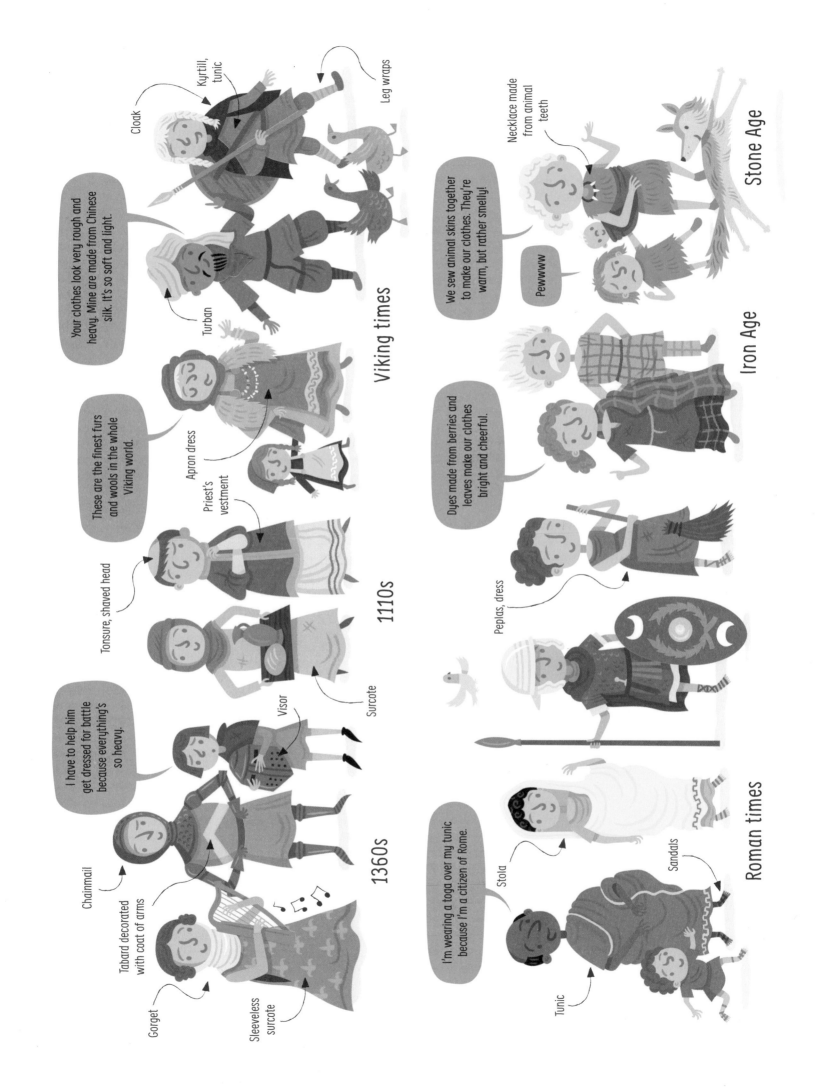

IRON-AGE HILLFORT

There was no town at all 2,300 years ago. People lived by farming the land. They made tools from iron and built their homes in hillforts to keep the group, known as a tribe, safe from attackers.

It used to be all forest in this valley.

Warriors with painted faces

Wooden frame

We've beaten the tribe from across the valley!

Woven strips of wood, called wattle.

This high fence and gate help keep out enemies.

Roundhouse

CLUCK

War chariot

These prisoners can do our hard work for us.

HONK!

HONK!

Each house has a fire in the middle for cooking and heating. Smoke from the fire escapes out of the thatched roof.

I want to be a great warrior when I grow up!

Grinding wheat to make flour

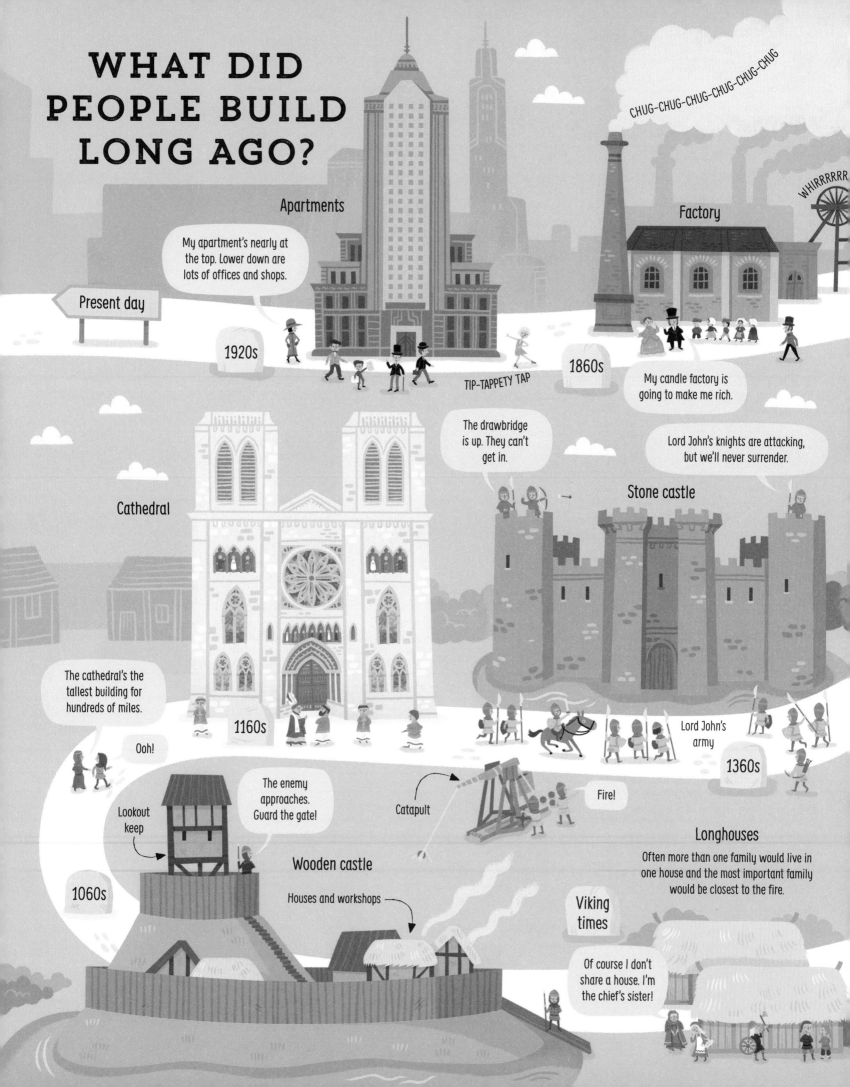

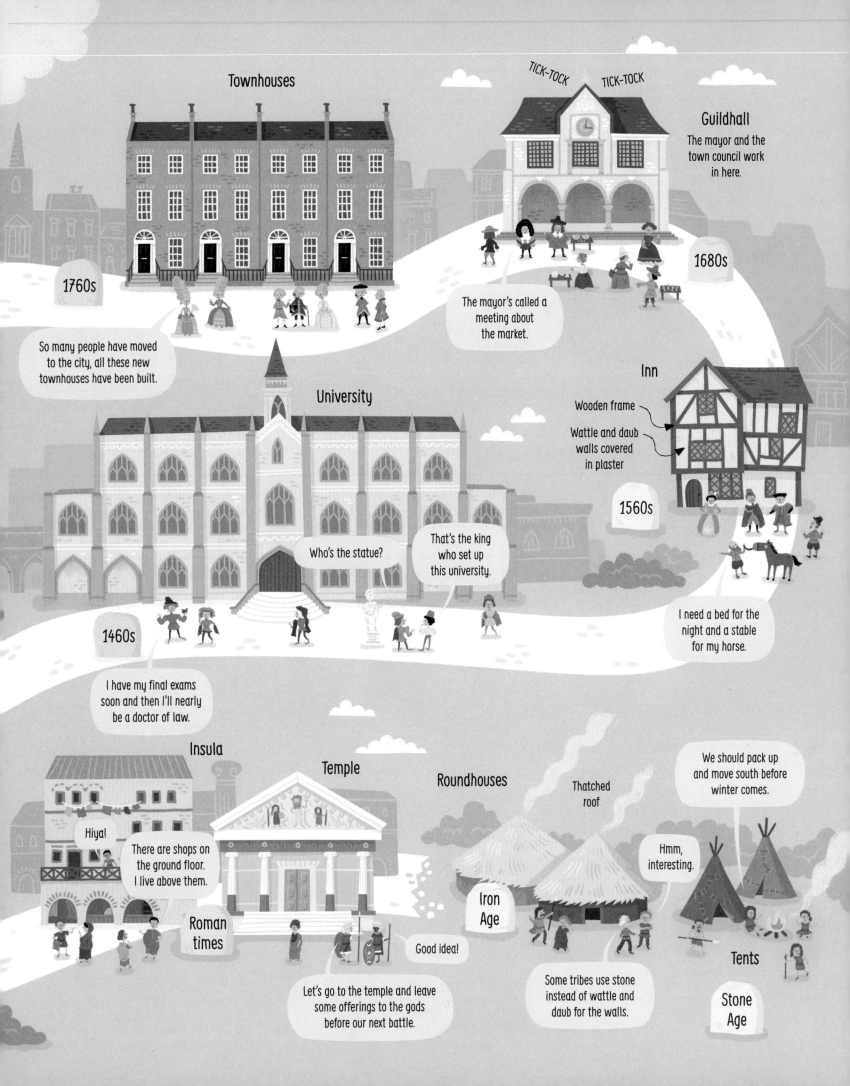

CAN YOU SPOT?

Look back at the scenes in the book. See if you can spot these things.

A man running late

A little girl chatting to a canary

A lady with a boat in her hair

A goose thief

A monkey dressed in red

A student washing

A servant dropping bread

A tiny statue

A leg wrestle

Two naughty children

A child tangled in yarn

A greedy dog

Usborne Quicklinks

For links to websites where you can find out more about how people lived long ago, go to the Usborne Quicklinks website at www.usborne.com/quicklinks and enter the keywords 'Big Picture Book of Long Ago'.
Please read our internet safety guidelines at the Usborne Quicklinks website.
We recommend that children are supervised while using the internet.

Historical consultant: Dr. Anne Millard Managing editor: Ruth Brocklehurst
Managing designer: Nicola Butler Digital manipulation: Nick Wakeford